EMMANUEL JOSEPH

The Social Contract in the Boardroom, Bridging Politics, Society, and Profit

Copyright © 2025 by Emmanuel Joseph

All rights reserved. No part of this publication may be reproduced, stored or transmitted in any form or by any means, electronic, mechanical, photocopying, recording, scanning, or otherwise without written permission from the publisher. It is illegal to copy this book, post it to a website, or distribute it by any other means without permission.

First edition

This book was professionally typeset on Reedsy. Find out more at reedsy.com

Contents

1 Chapter 1: The Evolution of Corporate Governance   1
2 Chapter 2: The Intersection of Politics and Business   3
3 Chapter 3: Corporate Social Responsibility (CSR)   5
4 Chapter 4: The Role of the Board in Ethical Decision-Making   7
5 Chapter 5: Stakeholder Theory in Practice   9
6 Chapter 6: Corporate Governance and Environmental...   10
7 Chapter 7: Diversity and Inclusion in the Boardroom   12
8 Chapter 8: The Digital Transformation of Corporate...   14
9 Chapter 9: Crisis Management and Board Leadership   16
10 Chapter 10: Measuring and Reporting Social Impact   18
11 Chapter 11: The Future of Corporate Governance   20
12 Chapter 12: Bridging the Gap Between Politics, Society, and...   22
13 Chapter 13: The Role of Corporate Culture in Governance   24
14 Chapter 14: The Impact of Globalization on Corporate...   25
15 Chapter 15: The Role of Technology in Enhancing Board...   26
16 Chapter 16: Ethical Leadership in the Digital Age   27
17 Chapter 17: The Future of Work and Corporate Governance   28

1

Chapter 1: The Evolution of Corporate Governance

In the early days of commerce, business leaders operated with little oversight, guided primarily by profit motives. The industrial revolution saw the birth of corporations, leading to the necessity for structured governance. As industries expanded, the need for a systematic approach to overseeing operations became evident. Companies grew in influence, transforming the way boardrooms operated, with an increasing focus on ethical practices.

The role of corporate boards evolved significantly over time. Initially, they functioned as mere watchdogs, ensuring that executives did not stray from their profit-driven paths. However, as societal expectations began to shift, the responsibilities of board members expanded. They became stewards of ethical business practices, tasked with ensuring transparency and accountability. This chapter delves into the historical context of corporate governance, illustrating the gradual transformation in boardroom dynamics. The emphasis shifted from pure profitability to incorporating broader societal values.

The modern-day emphasis on transparency, accountability, and social responsibility can be traced back to several key developments. Regulatory reforms, driven by high-profile corporate scandals, played a crucial role. Governments and regulatory bodies worldwide introduced stringent measures to ensure companies operated ethically and transparently. These reforms demanded that boards adopt a more proactive role in overseeing operations, leading to the rise of independent directors and the establishment of audit committees. This evolution marked a significant departure from the laissez-faire approach of the past, highlighting the growing recognition of the interconnectedness between business practices and societal well-being.

In recent decades, the concept of corporate governance has continued to evolve. The rise of stakeholder theory, which advocates for considering the interests of all stakeholders, not just shareholders, has gained traction. This shift has been driven by a growing recognition that businesses must operate in harmony with their communities and the environment. As companies embrace this holistic approach, boardrooms are becoming more diverse and inclusive, reflecting the broader societal commitment to equity and sustainability. The evolution of corporate governance is a testament to the dynamic interplay between business practices and societal values, highlighting the importance of ethical leadership in shaping the future of commerce.

2

Chapter 2: The Intersection of Politics and Business

The relationship between politics and business is intricate and multifaceted. Political policies shape the business environment, influencing factors such as taxation, regulation, and trade. Conversely, businesses can impact political agendas through lobbying, donations, and advocacy. This symbiotic relationship is fundamental to understanding how corporations operate within the broader societal context.

One of the most notable examples of this intersection is the influence of corporate lobbying. Companies often lobby for favorable regulations or policies that can benefit their operations. While this practice can lead to positive outcomes, such as job creation and economic growth, it also raises ethical questions. The balance between legitimate advocacy and undue influence is delicate, and boards must navigate this terrain with caution. The chapter provides case studies of how businesses have successfully and ethically engaged in lobbying, highlighting the importance of transparency and accountability.

Political stability is another critical factor that influences business operations. Companies thrive in stable environments where policies are predictable and the rule of law is upheld. Conversely, political instability can create uncertainty, making it challenging for businesses to plan and invest. This chapter explores how businesses navigate political risks, including strategies for mitigating potential disruptions. Examples from various industries illustrate how proactive engagement with political stakeholders can create a more favorable operating environment.

Finally, the chapter examines the ethical implications of corporate political involvement. While businesses have a right to advocate for their interests, they must do so responsibly. Boards play a crucial role in ensuring that their political activities align with the company's values and do not compromise its integrity. The discussion extends to the importance of ethical leadership and the role of regulatory bodies in maintaining a fair and transparent political-business interface.

3

Chapter 3: Corporate Social Responsibility (CSR)

As public awareness of social issues grows, so does the demand for businesses to contribute positively to society. Corporate Social Responsibility (CSR) has become a vital component of modern business practices, reflecting the need for companies to go beyond profit-making and address societal challenges.

CSR encompasses a wide range of initiatives, from philanthropic efforts to sustainable business practices. This chapter defines CSR and its significance in today's corporate world. We explore various models of CSR, such as the Triple Bottom Line, which emphasizes economic, social, and environmental performance. By integrating these elements into their strategies, companies can enhance their reputation and build stronger relationships with stakeholders.

Real-world examples demonstrate how businesses have successfully implemented CSR initiatives. For instance, companies that invest in renewable energy or support community development projects can create positive social impacts while also driving business growth. The chapter highlights the benefits of CSR, including increased customer loyalty, improved employee engagement, and enhanced brand reputation.

However, implementing effective CSR strategies is not without challenges.

Boards must ensure that their CSR initiatives are genuine and aligned with the company's core values. The chapter discusses the importance of transparency in reporting CSR activities and the role of board members in overseeing these efforts. By fostering a culture of social responsibility, boards can help companies achieve long-term success while contributing to the greater good.

4

Chapter 4: The Role of the Board in Ethical Decision-Making

Ethical dilemmas are an inevitable part of business operations, and the board's role in navigating these challenges is crucial. Boards are responsible for setting the ethical tone of the organization, ensuring that business practices align with societal values and regulatory standards.

This chapter focuses on the processes through which boards can foster a culture of integrity. Ethical leadership starts at the top, with board members serving as role models for the entire organization. By establishing clear ethical guidelines and decision-making frameworks, boards can guide executives and employees in making responsible choices.

Case studies illustrate both successes and failures in ethical governance. Examples of companies that have faced ethical crises reveal the consequences of poor decision-making and the steps taken to rectify such situations. These case studies underscore the importance of proactive ethical leadership and the need for continuous monitoring and improvement.

The chapter also covers the impact of regulatory bodies in enforcing ethical standards. Boards must ensure compliance with laws and regulations, while also addressing the ethical expectations of stakeholders. This dual responsibility requires a comprehensive approach to governance, integrating ethical considerations into all aspects of business operations. By doing so, boards can build trust and credibility, fostering a sustainable and ethical business environment.

5

Chapter 5: Stakeholder Theory in Practice

Stakeholder theory posits that businesses should prioritize the interests of all stakeholders, not just shareholders. This approach recognizes that companies have responsibilities to a wide range of individuals and groups, including employees, customers, suppliers, and the community.

This chapter delves into the practical application of stakeholder theory in the boardroom. We discuss methods for identifying and engaging with various stakeholder groups, emphasizing the importance of understanding their needs and expectations. By adopting a stakeholder-oriented strategy, companies can create more sustainable and equitable business practices.

Real-world examples demonstrate the benefits of stakeholder engagement. Companies that actively involve stakeholders in decision-making processes can build stronger relationships and achieve better outcomes. For instance, engaging with employees can lead to improved job satisfaction and productivity, while collaborating with suppliers can enhance supply chain resilience.

The chapter also explores the challenges boards face in balancing conflicting stakeholder interests. Conflicts may arise when the interests of one group are at odds with those of another. Boards must navigate these conflicts carefully, seeking solutions that align with the company's values and long-term goals. Strategies for mitigating conflicts and fostering collaboration are discussed, highlighting the importance of effective communication and transparency.

6

Chapter 6: Corporate Governance and Environmental Sustainability

Environmental sustainability has become a crucial aspect of corporate governance. As society grapples with climate change and environmental degradation, the role of businesses in promoting sustainability has never been more critical. This chapter examines the board's role in integrating sustainability into business strategies, highlighting the importance of the triple bottom line—people, planet, and profit.

The concept of the triple bottom line emphasizes the need for businesses to balance economic performance with social and environmental responsibility. Boards play a pivotal role in ensuring that their companies adopt sustainable practices that minimize environmental impact. This includes setting ambitious sustainability goals, monitoring progress, and holding executives accountable for achieving these targets. By prioritizing sustainability, boards can drive long-term value creation and build resilient organizations.

Real-world examples of companies that have successfully integrated sustainability into their operations provide valuable insights. For instance, companies that invest in renewable energy, reduce waste, and promote circular economy principles can significantly reduce their environmental footprint. These initiatives not only benefit the planet but also enhance a company's reputation and attract environmentally conscious consumers and investors.

Regulatory frameworks play a crucial role in shaping corporate sustainability efforts. Boards must ensure compliance with environmental laws and regulations while also going beyond minimum requirements to demonstrate leadership in sustainability. This chapter discusses the importance of proactive engagement with regulators and stakeholders to drive meaningful change. By championing sustainability, boards can position their companies as industry leaders and contribute to a more sustainable future.

7

Chapter 7: Diversity and Inclusion in the Boardroom

Diversity and inclusion are essential for fostering innovative and resilient organizations. A diverse board brings a wealth of perspectives, experiences, and ideas, enhancing decision-making and driving better business outcomes. This chapter discusses the importance of diverse board composition and the benefits of including individuals from varied backgrounds.

Boards that prioritize diversity and inclusion are better equipped to navigate complex challenges and seize new opportunities. Research has shown that diverse teams are more innovative, make better decisions, and achieve higher financial performance. This chapter explores strategies for promoting diversity and inclusion within the boardroom, including recruitment practices, mentorship programs, and inclusive leadership development.

Successful examples from leading companies highlight the positive impact of diversity and inclusion initiatives. Companies that actively promote diversity and create inclusive cultures can attract top talent, foster employee engagement, and build stronger relationships with stakeholders. The chapter also addresses the challenges and resistance to diversity initiatives, offering practical solutions for overcoming these obstacles.

Boards play a critical role in setting the tone for diversity and inclusion

CHAPTER 7: DIVERSITY AND INCLUSION IN THE BOARDROOM

across the organization. By championing inclusive practices and holding executives accountable, boards can drive meaningful change and create environments where all individuals can thrive. This chapter emphasizes the importance of continuous learning and adaptation in fostering diverse and inclusive boardrooms.

8

Chapter 8: The Digital Transformation of Corporate Governance

The digital age has revolutionized corporate governance, reshaping how boards operate and make decisions. This chapter explores the impact of digital transformation on corporate governance, highlighting the opportunities and challenges presented by new technologies.

Digital tools enhance transparency, efficiency, and accountability in governance processes. Boards can leverage technology to access real-time data, streamline decision-making, and improve communication with stakeholders. For example, digital dashboards and analytics tools provide valuable insights into company performance, enabling boards to make informed decisions quickly and effectively.

Successful digital transformation initiatives illustrate how boards can harness technology to drive innovation and stay competitive. Companies that embrace digital transformation can optimize operations, enhance customer experiences, and create new revenue streams. However, the digital landscape also presents risks and challenges, including cybersecurity threats and data privacy concerns.

The chapter discusses the importance of robust cybersecurity measures and the board's role in overseeing digital risks. Boards must ensure that their companies adopt best practices for data protection and incident response, safeguarding sensitive information and maintaining stakeholder trust. By embracing digital transformation, boards can position their companies for long-term success in an increasingly digital world.

9

Chapter 9: Crisis Management and Board Leadership

Crisis management is a critical aspect of corporate governance, requiring boards to lead organizations through challenging times with resilience and integrity. This chapter examines the board's role in crisis management, emphasizing the principles of effective leadership and proactive risk assessment.

Crisis scenarios can range from financial downturns and natural disasters to reputational scandals and cybersecurity breaches. Boards must be prepared to respond swiftly and decisively, prioritizing transparent communication and stakeholder engagement. By establishing clear crisis management frameworks and protocols, boards can guide their companies through turbulence and emerge stronger.

Case studies of companies that have successfully navigated crises provide valuable lessons. These examples highlight the importance of resilience planning, including scenario analysis, contingency planning, and continuous monitoring of potential risks. Boards that prioritize crisis preparedness can mitigate the impact of disruptions and safeguard their companies' long-term viability.

The chapter also covers the board's responsibility in fostering a culture of resilience and adaptability. By promoting continuous learning and encouraging a proactive approach to risk management, boards can empower their organizations to thrive in the face of uncertainty. Effective crisis management requires collaboration, clear communication, and a steadfast commitment to ethical leadership.

10

Chapter 10: Measuring and Reporting Social Impact

Transparency in measuring and reporting social impact is vital for building trust with stakeholders and demonstrating a company's commitment to social responsibility. This chapter discusses the frameworks and metrics boards can use to evaluate and communicate their social and environmental performance.

Integrated reporting, which combines financial and non-financial information, provides a holistic view of an organization's impact. By adopting integrated reporting practices, boards can offer stakeholders a comprehensive understanding of how the company creates value across multiple dimensions. This approach enhances accountability and fosters greater stakeholder engagement.

Examples of companies with robust reporting practices showcase the benefits of transparent communication. Organizations that effectively measure and report their social impact can build stronger relationships with investors, customers, and employees. Transparent reporting also drives continuous improvement, enabling companies to identify areas for growth and innovation.

The chapter addresses the challenges boards face in adopting comprehensive reporting standards. These challenges include aligning reporting

CHAPTER 10: MEASURING AND REPORTING SOCIAL IMPACT

practices with global standards, ensuring data accuracy, and maintaining consistency across reporting periods. Strategies for overcoming these hurdles are discussed, emphasizing the importance of board leadership in driving transparent and accountable governance.

11

Chapter 11: The Future of Corporate Governance

The landscape of corporate governance is continuously evolving, shaped by emerging trends and future challenges. This chapter explores the future of corporate governance, highlighting the skills and qualities that will be essential for effective board leadership.

Agility and adaptability are increasingly important in navigating the complexities of the modern business environment. Boards must embrace continuous learning and development, staying abreast of regulatory changes, technological advancements, and shifting societal expectations. By fostering a culture of innovation and flexibility, boards can drive long-term success and resilience.

The chapter discusses the potential impact of emerging technologies on corporate governance. Artificial intelligence, blockchain, and other digital innovations have the potential to revolutionize governance processes, enhancing transparency and efficiency. Boards that proactively explore these technologies can stay ahead of the curve and capitalize on new opportunities.

Forward-looking scenarios envision the boardroom of the future, where diverse and inclusive leadership, advanced digital tools, and a commitment to sustainability drive governance practices. The chapter emphasizes the importance of collaboration and dialogue among all stakeholders in achieving this vision. By embracing forward-thinking governance, boards can shape the future of business and contribute to a more equitable and sustainable world.

12

Chapter 12: Bridging the Gap Between Politics, Society, and Profit

In the concluding chapter, we synthesize the key themes discussed throughout the book. We explore the ways in which boards can bridge the gap between politics, society, and profit, fostering a holistic approach to corporate governance. By aligning business strategies with societal values and political considerations, boards can drive sustainable growth and long-term success.

Collaboration and dialogue among all stakeholders are essential in achieving this vision. Boards must engage with political leaders, community representatives, and other stakeholders to understand their perspectives and build mutually beneficial relationships. By fostering open communication and transparency, boards can create a more inclusive and equitable business environment.

The chapter highlights the importance of ethical leadership and the board's role in setting the tone for responsible business practices. By championing social responsibility, environmental sustainability, and diversity and inclusion, boards can build resilient organizations that thrive in the face of change.

We conclude with a call to action for board members to embrace their role as stewards of ethical, inclusive, and forward-thinking organizations.

CHAPTER 12: BRIDGING THE GAP BETWEEN POLITICS, SOCIETY, AND...

By bridging the gap between politics, society, and profit, boards can drive positive change and contribute to a more sustainable and prosperous future.

13

Chapter 13: The Role of Corporate Culture in Governance

Corporate culture significantly influences governance practices and organizational success. This chapter explores the relationship between corporate culture and governance, highlighting the importance of fostering a positive and ethical culture. Boards play a crucial role in shaping and maintaining this culture by setting the tone from the top.

A strong corporate culture promotes ethical behavior, transparency, and accountability. It can drive employee engagement, enhance customer satisfaction, and improve overall business performance. This chapter discusses strategies for boards to cultivate and sustain a positive corporate culture. These include aligning corporate values with governance practices, promoting open communication, and recognizing and rewarding ethical behavior.

Real-world examples illustrate how companies with strong corporate cultures have achieved long-term success. Conversely, we examine cases where toxic cultures have led to significant challenges and failures. The chapter emphasizes the board's responsibility in addressing cultural issues and fostering an environment where all employees feel valued and empowered.

14

Chapter 14: The Impact of Globalization on Corporate Governance

Globalization has transformed the business landscape, creating new opportunities and challenges for corporate governance. This chapter examines the impact of globalization on governance practices, highlighting the need for boards to navigate complex international environments.

Operating in multiple countries requires boards to understand diverse regulatory frameworks, cultural norms, and market dynamics. This chapter explores strategies for managing global operations, including establishing robust governance structures, fostering cross-cultural understanding, and ensuring compliance with international regulations.

Case studies of multinational corporations provide insights into effective global governance practices. We also discuss the challenges boards face in balancing local and global considerations, such as managing supply chain risks, addressing human rights issues, and promoting environmental sustainability. The chapter emphasizes the importance of a global mindset and the board's role in driving responsible and sustainable business practices across borders.

15

Chapter 15: The Role of Technology in Enhancing Board Effectiveness

Technology has the potential to enhance board effectiveness by improving decision-making, communication, and oversight. This chapter explores the ways in which boards can leverage technology to drive better governance outcomes.

Digital tools, such as board portals, virtual meeting platforms, and data analytics, can streamline board processes and enhance collaboration. This chapter discusses the benefits of adopting these tools, including increased efficiency, real-time access to information, and improved transparency. We also explore the challenges of implementing new technologies, such as ensuring cybersecurity and managing the digital divide.

Examples of companies that have successfully integrated technology into their board practices provide valuable lessons. The chapter emphasizes the importance of continuous learning and adaptation, encouraging boards to stay abreast of technological advancements and explore innovative solutions to governance challenges.

16

Chapter 16: Ethical Leadership in the Digital Age

The digital age presents unique ethical challenges for corporate leaders. This chapter examines the role of ethical leadership in navigating these challenges, emphasizing the importance of integrity, accountability, and transparency.

Digital technologies, such as artificial intelligence, big data, and social media, raise ethical questions related to privacy, security, and fairness. Boards must ensure that their companies adopt responsible practices in the use of these technologies. This chapter explores the ethical considerations boards should take into account, including data protection, algorithmic bias, and the responsible use of AI.

Case studies highlight instances where companies have successfully addressed ethical issues in the digital age. We also discuss the importance of ethical leadership in fostering a culture of responsibility and trust. By prioritizing ethical considerations in their decision-making, boards can build resilient organizations that thrive in the digital era.

17

Chapter 17: The Future of Work and Corporate Governance

The future of work is evolving rapidly, driven by technological advancements, changing workforce demographics, and shifting societal expectations. This chapter explores the implications of these trends for corporate governance and the role of boards in shaping the future of work.

Remote work, gig economy, and automation are transforming traditional employment models. Boards must navigate these changes by adopting flexible and inclusive governance practices. This chapter discusses strategies for managing a diverse and dispersed workforce, promoting employee well-being, and ensuring fair labor practices.

Real-world examples demonstrate how companies are adapting to the future of work. We also explore the challenges boards face in addressing workforce issues, such as reskilling and upskilling, fostering diversity and inclusion, and managing the impacts of automation. The chapter emphasizes the importance of forward-thinking governance in preparing organizations for the future of work.

The Social Contract in the Boardroom: Bridging Politics, Society, and Profit

In an ever-evolving corporate landscape, the convergence of politics,

CHAPTER 17: THE FUTURE OF WORK AND CORPORATE GOVERNANCE

society, and profit has become more pronounced than ever. "The Social Contract in the Boardroom" navigates this intricate terrain, offering a comprehensive exploration of corporate governance through the lens of social responsibility and ethical leadership. This book delves into the dynamic interplay between businesses and their broader societal context, highlighting the essential role of corporate boards in fostering transparency, accountability, and sustainability.

Spanning 17 chapters, the book provides an in-depth examination of various aspects of corporate governance, from the historical evolution of boardroom dynamics to the practical application of stakeholder theory. Readers will gain insights into the ethical challenges faced by boards, the impact of globalization and digital transformation, and the importance of diversity and inclusion. The book also addresses the future of work and the emerging trends that will shape corporate governance in the years to come.

Through real-world examples and case studies, "The Social Contract in the Boardroom" illustrates how businesses can align their strategies with societal values and political considerations, driving sustainable growth and long-term success. By bridging the gap between politics, society, and profit, this book serves as a call to action for board members to embrace their role as stewards of ethical, inclusive, and forward-thinking organizations.

Ideal for corporate leaders, board members, and anyone interested in the intersection of business and society, this book provides a valuable roadmap for navigating the complexities of modern governance. Whether you are a seasoned executive or a newcomer to the boardroom, "The Social Contract in the Boardroom" offers essential insights and practical guidance for fostering a more equitable and sustainable future.

www.ingramcontent.com/pod-product-compliance
Lightning Source LLC
LaVergne TN
LVHW010444070526
838199LV00066B/6184